Boris the Bustard's
Birdie Buddies

Written by Rocky Salt
Illustrated by Fred Fieber

Published in the United Kingdom by

Rocky Salt
Steeple Langford, Salisbury, Wilts, SP3 4NQ

Content copyright © Rocky Salt, 2019
Illustrations copyright © Fred Fieber, 2019

First printed January 2019

Rocky Salt and Fred Fieber have also written and illustrated An Animalphabet.

ISBN 978-1-64204-653-3

To Hannah and my mother and father. Thank you.

A VOCET

Avocet

The first little poem on birds of the world
Concerns a bird whose beak is curled.
If you go down to the shore, you'll see
A bird as pretty as pretty can be.

A century ago there were none to be seen.
In England, sadly, it became a has-been.
But kindly folk and changes of ways
Mean, for the avocet, happy days.

So, shyly sifting the sea and the silt
This black and white beauty on tiny stilts
Graces our flats for all to see
Thanks to the efforts of the RSPB.

B USTARD

Bustard

Boris the bustard's a chunky lump;
20 kilos from beak to rump.
The heaviest birds that are able to fly;
It takes a lot to take to the sky.

In eighteen thirty-two the last was shot.
Now they're coming back, so worry not.
You see, Boris and his mates were good to eat,
Being so big, with plenty of meat.

In England they live on Salisbury Plain
And come from Russia or Spain, in the main.
So, If you go where the bustards run,
Take a sketchbook, a camera ... but not a gun.

CHICKEN

Chicken

Have you seen the Great Book of Chicken History?
Their book of folklore.
They call it Yolklore.
In the beginning, an egg was found
Just lying, right there on the ground.
No-one knows how it got to be there.
It just appeared out of thin air.
And out of this egg came the Great Mother Hen;
The kindest of birds. So kind to men.
Then from the clouds came a very deep voice
And it said, "Mother, I give you a choice.
You can have wings to fly and soar
Or you can have all this food right here on the floor."
Now Mother Hen was very hungry: oh, was she ever!
But sadly she wasn't really all that clever.
So she chose the food over the flying
And that's why now (and I'm really not lying)
They hang around us and live in coops
And often get made into lovely soups.
They don't use their wings - just their legs
And lay for us hundreds of eggs.

DRONGO

Drongo

The drongo's a great bird: it makes me smile.
It gets its food through deceit and guile.
It watches meerkats hunting for food
And then it does something very rude.
It makes a noise like a meerkat's alarm.
If they stay out, they'll come to harm.
So down their holes they all scamper
And the drongo pinches their picnic hamper.

E

LEPHANT BIRD

Elephant Bird

Deep in the forests of Madagascar
There lived a bird you'll no longer see.
It wouldn't matter if you had a fast car,
The bird has left the Malagasy.

A bird the size of a pachyderm
(That's an elephant to you and me.)
A million times the size of a worm.
Some as tall as ten foot three.

A half a ton when on the scales.
That's a lot of meat to you and me.
Almost as much as some small whales.
Precisely why they're history.

Just imagine if these birds could fly.
You'd see one coming and want to flee
As it swooped from the sky
..... and broke the tree.

F LAMINGO

Flamingo

They're pink and graceful, with legs so long
And live in flocks, thousands strong.
When danger threatens and they've got to go,
They fly. They flee. Just flaming go.

G ALAH

Galah

Look at you, you flamin' galah.
I see you everywhere in Australiah.
A Cockatoo is what you aah.
And you fly in groups - but not very fah.

There's not much difference 'tween mah and pah.
Her eyes are red and his are dahrk.
But your pink feathers make you a stah.
So, you're my fave. A big Hurraah!

HUMMINGBIRD

Hummingbird

Hummingbirds? Why are they called hummingbirds?
Do they hum because they've forgotten the words?
But it doesn't hum; It actually sings.
The hum you hear comes from its wings.

IBIS

Ibis

I bis, you bis,
He or she bisses
We and they all bis.

How do you bis?
Is it to kiss with your lips sealed tightly?
Or is it to miss someone ever so slightly?

The birds don't care; they don't know.
They just wade in ponds and bogs
Hoping to catch small fish or frogs.

The Egyptians had a god with the head of an ibis.
And he was in charge of magic and writing.
And settling arguments when people were fighting.

This sacred bird is a wonder to see,
So it matters not if you kiss or miss;
We all adore the lovely ibis.

J<small>AY</small>

Jay

I say! Is that a jay?
Hunting for berries and eating my cherries?
Chatting away? And what does it say?
"This is my tree. They're all for me."
"Cherries I'll eat, but you really can't beat
Acorns from oaks … and that's not all, folks;
If I find a beech, I'll scream and screech.
But I don't actually mind; I'll eat what I find.
Birds' eggs are nice and so are mice."
The jay's quite bright; a beautiful sight -
Pink and blue and black and white.
But did you know it's actually a crow?

KITE

Kite

The kite when it dives is very whizzy
And it soars in circles but is never dizzy
Its feathers flutter when on the wing
But if it's a kite, where's the string?

L YREBIRD

Lyrebird

Lyrebird, lyrebird tell me no lies.
I want the truth when I look in your eyes.
Why do you spell your lyre with a "Y"
When the liar I know is spelled with an "I"?

I'm not a liar. I'll put you at peace.
A lyre's a harp that comes from Greece.
When I lift my tail a little higher,
It looks just like an old Greek lyre.

But out in the bush, where I spend my days,
The noises I make will shock and amaze.
I copy the sounds that you'd all like;
From a mobile phone to a motor bike.
From the clicks and whirrs of a camera shutter
To the chainsaw used by a big log cutter.
The sounds I make will truly surprise
And, no, they're not real - they're actual lies.

M

ARABOU STORK

Marabou Stork

Have you ever seen a bird so vile?
It looks so ugly it makes me smile.
Its eating habits are pretty gruesome.
The stork and the vulture - a ghastly twosome.

On the African plains when animals die,
The storks plump down from the deep blue sky
They squabble with vultures for pride of place
To scoff all the scraps. There is no waste.

And that's not the only foul thing they do.
They cover their legs with their very own poo
To stop them catching any grisly germs,
Bacteria, viruses or wiggly worms.

But just 'cos they're ugly, we can't be mean.
They help to keep the countryside clean.
They're hard to like, I must confess
But they stop the place from becoming a mess.

NENE

Nene

One day, when I was a lad,
I went to a park with my dad.
I saw a goose down by the lake
And I thought my little heart would break.
A Hawaiian goose; so very rare.
30 left and one was there.
But thanks to a man, called Peter Scott
We've got two and a half thousand - and that's a lot!
Soon we'll have more - like in their heyday.
So, good luck to you, you lucky nene.

O STRICH

Ostrich

Ostriches and zebras are the best of friends.
Where you see one, you'll see the other.
The zebra, you see, has very poor vision,
But excellent hearing and sense of smell.
The ostrich, though, has a great, long neck
And, with very good eyes, it sees for miles.
So, out on the plains when danger lurks,
One of the two will warn the other.
Isn't it good to work together?
Why don't we try and do the same?

Penguin

Penguin

A wonky penguin on stumpy legs.
Walking's a laugh with such short pegs.
A fish or a bird? You tell me.
Swims like a fish. Flies like a tree.

Penguins live in the south, in the worst of weathers
And keep themselves warm by oiling their feathers.
Then under that
They've got some fat.
Blubber I call it and so can you.
Whales have got it and seals have, too.

They swim out to sea and love to catch fish.
Krill and squid make a tasty dish.
But they have to watch out when they're having their meals
Because penguins are tasty to leopard seals.

QUETZAL

Quetzal

Imagine a pigeon, sitting in a tree -
A bit grey; not much to see.
But what if you added a 3 foot tail
And painted it brightly - well, just the male.
A bright red chest and feathers so green
It's the most beautiful bird you've ever seen.

Quetzal's the name and that's quite funny.
In Guatemala the quetzal's the name of their money.
They use the quetzal to pay for things,
But it's made of paper and doesn't have wings.
Just imagine if we had these.
"Two loaves for a pigeon. Thank you - and please."

R AVEN

Raven

A charm of goldfinches, an exaltation of larks.
Such sweet names; they get top marks.
But an unkindness of ravens; that's not fair
For the cleverest of birds that fly in the air.
Dressed in black from claw to bill
(That bill will kill, you know it will.)
But the raven has a brain, you know.
When solving problems, it ain't slow.
It has an eye for a shiny thing.
So, keep an eye on all your bling.
They love a ring, a bangle, a bead.
Because it's shiny; not for greed.
If you're in the garden and you lose a jewel,
The raven will have it, but that's not cruel.

SPARROW

Sparrow

Cheer up. Cheer up.
The twittering chorus
Of thousands of birds.
The constant chatter
Outside my window
It made me glad
To be awake.
When I was a boy,
It was always there.
You didn't look at them.
You didn't listen to them.
But the clamour was there
Just filling the air.
It's only when the noise has gone
That you notice what we're missing.
Things have changed
For the lowly sparrow.
Where once the sparrow was found in thousands
We find them now in ones and twos
And I, for one, am very sad
Not to hear their cheerful chirrup.
Maybe one day they'll all come back.
And if they do, I promise I'll look
At their cheeky antics
And I'll listen, too.
Please come back.

TURKEY

Turkey

"You're a fine looking turkey.
What do you do for work - ey?"

"I get fat and never shirk - ey."

"That's a good job. And the food's a perk - ey."
I said with just a hint of a smirk - ey.

"But I'm a turkey with a quirk - ey.
Christmas doesn't even start to irk - me.
When I see the farmer starting to lurk - ey,
I simply go and hide in the mirk - ey.
The farmer usually goes berzerk - ey."

Then I said bye bye to the turkey
And off he went, with his neck all jerk - ey.

U

MBRELLA BIRD

Umbrella Bird

Up in the clouds, high in the trees
Lives a bird we rarely see.
It's about the size of one of our crows
Clinging to branches, using its toes.
It hops around from bough to bough
And makes a noise just like a cow.
Bright red skin adorns the male's chest.
It's called a wattle. And - it has a crest.
The crest, it makes him a handsome fellah
And looks just like a black umbrella.
But it's not there to give him shelter.
It's just for looks - what a belter!

Vulture

Vulture

The vulture's not pretty by any means
Some say ugly, but that's being mean.
It's the biggest and hungriest bird I've seen
And if something dies, it'll strip it clean.

They'll see something as soon as it dies
Because they've got such very good eyes.
Then down they'll swoop to join the flies.
It's not a nice sight;
I'll tell you no lies.

But out on the plains, they're in the right place.
If clean-up's the job, they're on the case.
They'll tidy the mess without humour or grace
And don't really care what you think of their face.

Woodpecker

Woodpecker

For constantly banging heads against trees,
Here are the things a woodpecker needs:
Good neck muscles and very strong bills
And a ready supply of headache pills.

X-PARROT

X-Parrot

Time to shed a tear.
Nothing to see here.
Just an empty page.
Polly's left the cage.

She's in a tree, up on a hill
Back at home in Brazil.
She flew through an open door.
The cage? The bars? Hers no more.

To keep her there was absurd.
We like to say, "Free as a bird".
So she's with her friends.
Don't be sad.
She's not alone.
That makes me glad.

Y ELLOWHAMMER

Yellowhammer

A little bit of bread and no cheese.
That's what I'd like. Please, pretty please.
This is the sound you hear on a walk
If you go up on the downs, all covered in chalk.
A splash of yellow on a branch over there
And then it's away, into the air.

Zebra Finch

Zebra Finch

Down by the banks of the billabong
The finches all meet in the shade of a tree
To see who's best in their singalong,
But who's the best? They'll never agree.
The noise to us is like constant chatter;
A babbling din; they all sound the same.
But to them, their song, it really does matter.
This is serious - it's not just a game.
The one who sings the very best song
Will have the best brood and pass on their genes.
The champion birds of the billabong.
The zebra finch bosses - the Kings and Queens.